Vitals

Vitals

Rosamund Small

Vitals
first published 2016 by
Scirocco Drama
An imprint of J. Gordon Shillingford Publishing Inc.

Scirocco Drama Editor: Glenda MacFarlane
Cover design by Terry Gallagher/Doowah Design.
Cover illustration by Chloe Cushman.
Author photo by Liam Coo.
Printed and bound in Canada on 100% post-consumer recycled paper.

We acknowledge the financial support of the Manitoba Arts Council and The Canada Council for the Arts for our publishing program.

Production inquiries should be addressed to:
Playwrights Guild of Canada
401 Richmond Street West, Suite 350
Toronto, ON M5V 3A8
Phone 416-703-0201
Fax 416-703-0059
info@playwrightsguild.ca

Library and Archives Canada Cataloguing in Publication

Small, Rosamund, author
Vitals / Rosamund Small.

A play.
ISBN 978-1-927922-24-8 (paperback)

I. Title.

PS8637.M353V58 2016 C812'.6 C2016-905006-8

J. Gordon Shillingford Publishing
P.O. Box 86, RPO Corydon Avenue, Winnipeg, MB Canada R3M 3S3

This play is dedicated to my parents,
Peter Small and Angela Carroll,
my sister Francesca Small,
and our dogs Poppy and Clive.

Acknowledgements

This play would not exist without the generosity and insight of Kaleigh O'Brien, Toronto paramedic and excellent friend. I can never thank Kaleigh enough for inspiring this writing, and supporting the script and production at every step. Thanks also to Todd Light, Evelyn Light and Charlotte Light.

Many thanks to the entire community of Toronto paramedics and emergency workers who supported the show in so many ways, and whose work and dedication continues to fascinate, astound and inspire me.

This project took a very large, very talented, intensely hard working village to come together. The production team, apprentices, the Heins family, who let us take over their house for months, everyone at Outside the March and Theatre Passe Muraille, and a thousand more friends and colleagues who lent us furniture, donated money or time, or told their friends about our show, all deserve more thanks than I can express.

All our collaborators deserve essays on my gratitude, but I will suffice here with brief shout-outs to the first three people to join me on this project: Katherine Cullen, for always going so far beyond reasonable expectations, for reading me the script aloud a thousand times, and for putting her immense heart and super sharp mind behind every breath of her performance. Djanet Sears, for encouraging me in her playwriting class to delve deeper into this piece and for putting unending hours into reading drafts and giving notes. And thanks to Mitchell Cushman, who asked to direct the show after reading seven pages of a first draft, and so far hasn't admitted that might have been a crazy decision. Mitch, you are my mentor, collaborator, favourite director and top notch friend. Thank you, thank you, thank you, thank you.

Our other chief collaborators on design and production—Sam, Anahita, Hanna, Shannon, Sebastien, Andrew, and Kat—went so far above and beyond for this show. Thank you for setting the bar so high and for taking every crazy idea and truly running with it, to such creative and beautiful results.

Also so many thanks to the Outside the March apprentices, without whom the production would not have been possible: Nicole Buscema, Zoe Danahy, Dana Deoraj, Ximena Huizi, Hannah Kaya, Dayna Miller, Rashida Shaw, Vanessa Spence, Jesse Watts, Jean Webb.

Also many thanks to John & Shella Heins, Tema Conter Memorial Trust, Andy McKim, Iris Turcott, Britta Johnson, Theatre Passe Muraille, Videofag, Alison Norwich, Ben Baker, Paul Williams, Cameron Laurie, the neighbours on Pearson, Graeme Rose, Daphne Bailie and Medicine in Film, Anika Johnson, Callan Furlong, Katie Housley, Ronalda Jones & Gary Furlong, Morgan Jones Phillips, Simon Bloom, Rob Kempson, Vivien Endicott-Douglas, Liam Coo, and Shifra Cooper.

Foreword

By Mitchell Cushman

You don't know what a call is
going to be like until you get there.

Vitals captivated me as soon as I read this very first line, in part because it aligns so closely with my hopes for what a night at the theatre can be—a truly unexpected event from the moment that you arrive.

Rosamund has written a solo show like none I have ever read or experienced. A haunting mosaic of a character study that dives deep into what it means to bear witness. My cousin is an EMS worker, and when Rosamund and I spoke with him in preparation for our production, he shared with us a mantra that I've since heard echoed by many of his colleagues: "It's not your emergency, it's *their* emergency."

And so in *Vitals* we get to know the paramedic at the centre of the play not through her own experiences, but through a host of intermediaries. Imperiled strangers in the night. Some pull through, some are too far-gone long before the essential eight minutes and fifty-nine seconds, but each encounter plays a formative part in sculpting the character of Anna.

At its core, to me *Vitals* is a story about the cost of offering help. We've all heard of the supposed ancient custom that says if you save someone's life, you are now responsible for that person. In all the research I've done, I can't find a cultural tradition that actually claims such a practice. Nevertheless, this trope continues to get recycled in art and culture, I would guess because there is something intuitive about it. It just *feels* true. Helping someone to remain in this world, (or preventing someone from leaving it)—how could that not come with some kind of cosmic charge? *Vitals* delves, beautifully and simply, into both the colossal weight and banal routine that make up the poles of working crisis after crisis, day after day.

Outside the March is an immersive theatre company, and as such we searched for ways to bring the audience as deeply as possible inside Anna's experience, both the truly exceptional and the hopelessly bureaucratic. We staged the show inside a three-story residential house (and in this I will be forever indebted to the Heins family). Every inch of the home was intricately designed to offer a distorted remembrance of the different calls Anna describes throughout the play, or the system that governs her protocol. The kitchen became overgrown like High Park, with soil filling nooks and crannies in every appliance and fixture; the bedroom became an intricately shrink-wrapped hotel room; a walk-in closet became a snow-filled shrine to a guy who had frozen himself like a snowman. But the mainframe of our world was a large file room, where a towering stack of cardboard boxes marked the attempts that Anna makes to try to document, and then expunge these various encounters from her psyche. Our aim was to offer an experience of journeying though Anna's mind, which matched the intensely intimate nature of the writing.

Throughout our production, we incorporated police scanner transmissions, broadcast live from the skipping heartbeat of Toronto—courtesy of an iPhone app that picks up emergency frequencies from all over the world. It felt important to include these nightly live transmissions, rather than use pre-recorded content: a sobering reminder of all the turmoil, all of the misfortunes, all of the emergencies that go part-and-parcel with living in any major city, as well as a tribute to all of the unsung heroes who respond to those in need.

Put simply—this play will hold a lot of imagination. Whether you stage *Vitals* in a small black box theatre, on a large proscenium, or in a found space, the play's wry humour, stark juxtaposition and boundless humanity will shine bright.

It was a true privilege to help bring Rosamund's intricate, compassionate and unflinchingly current writing to life—exhilarating to work on something that felt so connected to our here and now. I am thrilled that readers and theatre artists all over Canada and beyond will be able to connect with this thrilling script, and arrive at their own first response.

Mitchell Cushman is a director, playwright, and dramaturge based in Toronto, and the founding Artistic Director of Outside the March. *The company's production of* Vitals *received the 2014 Dora Awards for Outstanding Independent Production and Outstanding New Play.*

www.outsidethemarch.ca

Rosamund Small

Rosamund Small is the Playwright-in-Residence of Outside the March. Her upcoming project with OtM—*TomorrowLove*™—is an immersive theatrical experience about love, technology and the future. It opens in Toronto in fall 2016.

Vitals was honoured with Dora Mavor Moore awards for Outstanding Production and Outstanding New Play, as well as the Nora Epstein National Literary Award and the JP Bickell Award for Drama. *Vitals* was adapted by Rosamund into an independent film, produced by Outside the March as an immersive filmgoing experience in collaboration with cinematographer Mike McLaughlin.

Rosamund also collaborates regularly on multidisciplinary work with ballet choreographer Robert Binet, most recently with the National Ballet of Canada, and his new international ballet company Wild Space.

Rosamund spent four years in artistic programming with the Paprika Festival, and loves collaborating with young artists. Currently, Rosamund is busy creating a new large-scale immersive show commissioned by Rosedale Heights School of the Arts for their students to produce and perform.

Other playwriting credits include *Sleep* (Wrecking Ball 17, 2014), *Genesis & Other Stories* (Aim for the Tangent, 2013) and *Performing Occupy Toronto* (Docket Theatre, 2012).

Rosamund studied Theatre and Sexual Diversity Studies at the University of Toronto. She is a member of the Soulpepper Academy.

Production History

Originally produced by Outside the March in May 2014. Production sponsored by Theatre Passe Muraille. A part of Passe Muraille's 2013/2014 Season. Originally performed in the home of the Heins family in Toronto.

Written by Rosamund Small
Directed by Mitchell Cushman

Dramaturgy by Djanet Sears
Production Design by Anahita Dehbonehie
Sound Design by Samuel Sholdice
Costume Design by Shannon Lea Doyle
Paramedic Consultant Kaleigh O'Brien
Set and Lighting Design Assistant Hanna Puley

With Katherine Cullen as Anna

Performer and Production Apprentices:

Nicole Buscema (Producing team)
Zoe Danahy (Producing team)
Dana Deoraj (Design team)
Ximena Huizi (Design team)
Hannah Kaya (Assistant Director)
Dayna Miller (Design team)
Rashida Shaw (Design team)
Vanessa Spence (Assistant Costume Designer)
Jesse Watts (Producing team)
Jean Webb (Playwright Associate and Design team)

With Sebastien Heins as the Voice of the Dispatcher
Jesse Watts as The Man
And Sagwa Heins as The Dog

PRODUCTION TEAM

Producer – Katherine Devlin Rosenfeld
Stage Manager – Andrew Morris
Production Manager – Jason Golinsky
Audience Liaison – Sebastien Heins
Associate Producer – Amy Keating
Theatre Passe Muraille Liaison – Jenn Sartor

Photography – Sebastien Heins
Video – Sebastien Heins and Lee Bremer
Poster Illustration and Design by Chloe Cushman
Graphic Design – Simon Bloom

Development for the writing of *Vitals* was supported by the Ontario Arts Council Theatre Creators Reserve, recommended by The Summerworks Festival, Factory Theatre and Theatre Passe Muraille.

The Outside the March 2014 Production was supported by the Ontario Arts Council, Toronto Arts Council, and Canada Council for the Arts.

Playwright's Notes

Vitals is the story of a woman who wants to help others, but ends up fighting for her own life. Other than this, it is very open to interpretation. I consider it an open text, in the sense that there is no one correct vision for staging it. The only essential thing is that however the piece is produced, it should be a journey through Anna's mind. Maybe this is as simple as one performer facing the audience, and sharing her story. Or maybe this is an adventure, a mysterious journey the audience walks through, until they follow Anna into her darkest secrets.

There is one clear pitfall to avoid when staging, performing or even just imagining this story: a bad interpretation of this script could easily begin with a traumatized and devastated woman, and go nowhere. Anna must meet us initially with a sense of pride, strength and humour. She is not weak. She survived for years doing a very difficult job effectively. She is bright, she loves her work, and she finds purpose in the challenges of her day-to-day experiences. It is just as important to find the grounded, working, fulfilled Anna at the beginning, as it is to find the shocked, overburdened Anna near the end of the story. That journey should be the focus of any performers and directors interested in bringing this play to life, and I hope it gives context for the imagination of anyone approaching this work as a reader.

Visual Ideas For The Staging of This Play

A city house. It is cluttered in parts, filled with a mountain of odds and ends: furniture, books, TVs, carpets, clothing, medical supplies, board games, mops, books, lawnmowers, globes, fans, and so forth. There is feeling that the house has become too full, as though too many people live in the house, and all of them are very messy. There are lots and lots and lots of phones, including cell phones and land lines, and the hundred land line phone cords crisscross through the space, wrapped around the mountains of objects, and tangling above Anna's head.

Alternatively, this play could be set in an ambulance. A theatre set could become the cramped, tiny space that paramedics share with patients in crisis.

This play could also be in an empty space, with nothing but Anna and her memories. Her memories could be shadows, projections or… just described by a performer, for us to imagine.

Sound Ideas For This Play

Tchaikovsky's 1812. Traffic, subway sounds (the sound of the train, the sound of the crackling TTC announcements, the door chimes). Sounds of a city. Traffic. Sirens. Motors. Dogs. Heartbeats. Doors opening and closing. Sound of knocking on doors. The regular beep of a heart monitor. Wolves.

Character

ANNA, *A paramedic.*

(A 911 dispatcher's voice is also heard from a phone).

Scene

A big city.

A single moment in time, present day.

Prologue

Ring ring. Ring ring.

A call connects. Much of it is interrupted by static and the quiet sound of a dog barking, a wolf howling, banging, more static.

DISPATCHER: 911. What's your emergency? Do you require Fire? Police? Ambulance?... What is your emergency?... OK, can you speak up? What's the address?

151 Pearson. Help is on its way. They'll be there in a moment—OK... And do you have any pets? Help is coming. Can you unlock the door? OK. 151 Pearson, that's a house right? Don't worry the ambulance is on its way—

Dispatcher is cut off. We see ANNA. She is in civilian clothes. Her hands are covered in blood.

ANNA: I should have been a veterinarian. People are terrible.

Chapter One

A shift. We are in the world of ANNA's mind. ANNA casually cleans the blood off her hands, and changes into her medic uniform. She begins to tell us about her job.

ANNA: You don't know what a call is going to be like until you get there. You take what they give you, like: hemorrhage. And you think of what you'll do depending on what kind of hemorrhage. Could be anything. But you don't know. You can only try to think of all the different things while you're driving like: miscarriage, aneurysm… hemophilia, maybe. And then when you get there, look really carefully and decide what you're going to do. Fast. That's if you're in the back and somebody else is doing the driving. You can't do that thinking while you're the one driving the ambulance to a scene. Cause even though driving the ambulance is the break—it's not hard, not like the job—it's still full of things. Full of issues. Like, people jaywalk. Which every time I'm like—really? You couldn't wait ten seconds for the ambulance to pass you? We go faster than anybody else, just wait. But people jaywalk. They just want to rush into things, and they don't seem to realize that *we* are the ones in a rush, we are 911, we are going somewhere because it's an emergency. And people also flag us down. And if we get flagged down, no matter what, we have to stop. Even on a critical call, we have to stop and assess. 'Cause it could be a heart attack. So we can be on our way to a fire—this happens, it happened when we were literally going to an apartment building on fire—And we got flagged down by a guy who was like—"I had dental surgery, it really hurts. Give me a ride to the hospital." I'm not a cab. I have to go to places that are critical, like places that are on fire. Or to see people who are coughing up blood. I can't help you right now. Don't flag me down because your tooth hurts. Pain is not urgent, dead people are urgent. I have to explain that a lot. Well, in a way, actually, dead people aren't urgent, only dying people are urgent. Dead people are just... clean up.

This one time... I wasn't driving, the other guy was driving—but we were on the way to a call from Castle Frank somebody had called from a pay phone on the platform said "I'm going to hurt myself, come get me" and then he hung up . So we're on the way to Castle Frank Station, thinking about the TTC stuff you have to worry about: Are there people on the platform? Did they stop the trains going to the station already? It's rush hour, how busy is the station going to be? We're in sight of the subway, on Bloor, sirens on, we can literally see the station and we get flagged down by this guy in a Leafs Jersey waving a red baseball cap. We pull over and he says "My arm hurts. I think it's broken. Please give me some codeine." Really, man? You couldn't take a cab to the hospital, we had the sirens on! Then the new call comes in and it's: *Man has made contact with train*. Which is dumb, but that means the guy at Castle Frank jumped and... made contact, obviously. So we missed it. Guy with a broken arm hears this and says "Well, that's the fucking TTC for you. Government doesn't have its shit together. Huge problems in this city, wolves everywhere, wolves in the transit system." And we have to be like, "OK, fine, but what happened, how did you break your arm?—" And the guy's like "the wolves have started to migrate across Sherbourne and they follow me around—" something or something, anyway, we're like "no, no wolves, no wolves, let's just take you to the hospital" but then he just ran away across Bloor. Well, told us to go fuck ourselves, and then ran away. Huge waste of time. We missed our jumper, and had to go to Castle Frank to clean him up. Or actually—that was a weird call, we didn't end up having anything to clean.

There's a lot of time pressure on TTC stuff—to keep moving, let the track open. So you have to work fast. Right away—back the train up, grab the body parts, you know… move. Go. Hurry. But don't drop anything. Then there's the basket and the freezer and everything and it's pretty high pressure, so we go in all ready, all prepared. The people are evacuated, we back the train up and then… nothing. The conductor is like, "I hit somebody, I know I hit somebody. I did!" But we look and we look and there's just nothing there. Not a piece of the guy is there. They roll the train right back but there's just no body. And we go crazy like, *Did he survive? Did he walk further down the track?* We're all wandering around like idiots, walking through the tunnel from Castle Frank to the bridge over the Don Valley. And here I am thinking: Oh, he didn't die. So he must've walked down the tunnel to the open bit and jumped into the Don. You can't jump from the bridge now cause of the fence-thing. But I thought this guy maybe jumped actually from the subway tracks under the bridge, into the Don. And that's horrible for the people driving in the Don to see, but a little part of me was like… how did he think of that? That's… clever. But they searched in the Don and… no body.

They play classical music at the subways on the upper platform bit to stop people from loitering. So when I think of the jumper I remember trying to like… search for the decapitated corpse and there's like… Tchaikovsky playing over us, like, soundtrack to the missing man. Anthem of the disappearing man. You know…

ANNA hums Tchaikovsky's 1812.

…it was super-dramatic. Weird stuff does happen on calls, all the time, but the jumper was kind of special, because the conductor was like, "I hit someone. I know I hit someone." And he was totally calm and normal but... certain. But we didn't find him. We never found the jumper.

Chapter Two

Gory things don't bother me at all really. Just the calls where people are.... mean to each other. The rapes and stuff. Those ones I don't like. The suicides are hard but not... that hard. It might be better if we had a decent psychologist. Our guy is awful, like, just really... he just brings snacks. That's it. Literally that is his entire job, apparently. And it's just like a joke—like, if you didn't have time to get lunch that day, call Psych. Dr. Wincheski will bring you a cookie. He, I don't know, I think he just has some weird crush on me or something 'cause he called me once, after the Scotiabank guy, and I was like: I'm fine. Because I was. Like I said, suicides aren't that bad, but after the Scotiabank guy he was like: "I really think you should talk to somebody." So we made this weird appointment and he asked—"Do you feel traumatized?" Right off the bat. And I was like: OK, I'm not a psychologist, but maybe you should be more subtle with your questions. And he's just waiting for me to answer while he keeps eating this enormous muffin. It was clearly his lunch. And he gets breaks. I don't know why he was always eating when he talked to people. And it was so pointless, he was just trying really hard to impress me with his empathy. Which, in the first place, I didn't need... didn't need it for that anyway.

But really suicides don't bother me so much. I'm glad when we can save them—intubate, cut the rope in time, restart their hearts, even talk them down from the roof of a building or whatever. A lot of people are happy that it didn't work, a lot of people are happy to be saved, and have a second chance. And it is nice, to see that. But it's not always possible… I do my best. But when they do die… you can't get too upset. They got what they wanted, you know? Their wish was fulfilled, right?

They are fucked sometimes, though. Like the guy who hanged himself in High Park from like, the *tallest* tree. He climbed the tallest tree and we had to get a cherry picker thing, because how else? It's the tallest tree in High Park. I don't even know how he climbed, or… you can't ask why. There is no why for suicides. That tree is in a bit of the park that is full of alive stuff: squirrels and rabbits and there's fish in the water right there. Maybe that's why he wanted to do it there. It's a nice bit of the city. I remember thinking… kind of morbid, but I thought… I should really come back here, High Park is really beautiful. That was a long day and when I got home I was making eggs and I kept thinking I saw him hanging from the corner of my eye. That's when I started realizing I have to make time to eat at work or I'm going to start seeing dead people in my kitchen.

One… it was called in as a hemorrhage at a yoga studio so I figured it must be a maternity class and I was going through in my mind all the different situations: Is she having the baby? Is she losing the baby? What do I do depending on what trimester it is… But I get there and, first of all, it's weirdly calm, like the studio is totally zen. There's zen music playing, and the receptionist just looks at me—completely normal—and says "He's in the back." First of all, *he*? Secondly, why is she so relaxed? And I go back there, and there are candles everywhere. And music still… and the guy at the back was the guy who owned the place. He had cut himself all over his legs, one long one down his arms and then a bunch from side to side. And he just lay down in his totally zen studio in this enormous pool of blood. And the receptionist seemed so calm. It was so weird. Yeah, he actually lived, so I don't know—I guess he's still teaching people yoga.

I think the Frosty guy was maybe the total weirdest. It was Christmas Day, 9 AM. This guy was wearing a huge kind of.... not hard plastic but, cellophane, slightly sort of opaque snowman outfit. I guess he put on his Frosty head with the carrot nose and the top hat and stuff, and he sat on a lawn chair at the end of his garden in the snow, right by the road, and took a bunch of pills. And he died. And it's Christmas morning, so people are going to church or whatever, going out to see the decorations and... the Frosty costume is kind of see-through, right? So children are walking by and being like..."there's a real guy in that snowman... Wow, he is totally not moving at all...." But that doesn't bother me, I'm not going to.... worry about Frosty. So he wanted to die as Frosty, who cares? At a certain point. I don't know...the guy... made a... statement. Not a clear statement. But you have to think it meant something to him.

A lot of people try to kill themselves at work. Yoga guy but also... hotels, oh my God, a lot of people at hotels in general, but one maid really went hard, drank a ton of clorox in a super fancy hotel room. Died right away. The guest came in to find her there in his bed. In your *bed!* On your *vacation.* And swimming pools, that's mostly accidents, but one lifeguard for sure meant to die in the pool. The offices aren't super memorable. But yeah, a lot of people at work. One time it was a nanny, that was sad, I remember her. This older woman from the Philippines. She did it in her room, which I guess counts as being at work. She lived at her work. She did it somewhere the kids couldn't find her. She was definitely being responsible, I think. I remember I wondered just for a second why she didn't leave her note in English, then I was like, oh, *It's not in English because it's for her actual family, in the Phillipines. Obviously*. But the Scotiabank guy was weird, in the bathroom of the Scotia building. He was a banker, a super-high-up banker. That's the one I had that stupid Psych meeting about. There was money everywhere, that was one of the weird things. And… he didn't miss, he didn't really miss, he shot himself in the head. But he missed his brain stem. So even though there's skull and brain matter everywhere and it's literally on the ceiling. I still had to… it's the law I had to try to revive him 'cause technically, there's nothing wrong with his respiratory system, he was still breathing. But, like, that's stupid. I was covered in… *him*, essentially, his brain. But his lungs are still—

(Takes a breath, illustrating lungs still breathing with her hands.)

—but I had his brain on… me so… it was so pointless. That's what was dumb, we shouldn't have to—we just needed somebody to call it, really. And right after that, like very soon after the Scotiabank guy I had to go to City Hall to do this thing about voting. There were all these city workers, a garbage man and a nurse and I was like *The Paramedic Who Votes!* Big smile. And someone was like, "You have some gum on your shoe." And I just tried to shrug it off, like "Oh thanks." But it was, like, you know…

Dr. Winchevski at Psych asked me: Do you feel traumatized? And I was like… "I don't like to chew gum anymore. I don't want gum in my mouth now, it looks to me like… a bit of a person. Otherwise I'm good."

The only ones that… well, no, the teenagers, sometimes… the teenage girls… that's hard. That bothers me. They never mean for it to work, that's the thing. But then, it usually doesn't work, they're usually fine, it's just....you know... them trying it out. Seeing if anyone would miss them. They take pills. We collect them, Emerg pumps their stomachs. One girl said the stomach pumping... she said it helped her lose weight. And that made her feel like living, I guess. And we send them to Psych to like... What does Psych do? Give them muffins, I guess.

One family... we found their daughter. She'd taken pills and changed her mind, called us... she's like... thirteen. It's not serious, it's barely anything, she could have fucked up her kidneys, but she's not dying. She's not—well, anyone can be dying without you noticing right away but—this girl is fine. But even so like that is kind of... she did try to kill herself. And her parents were just like... "oh yeah, she said she would do that." Like, "she did say she would kill herself. We didn't want to indulge it... she's the youngest, you know how that is." ...I don't know how that is. I don't know how that makes it a non-issue. But I guess the good thing is—she didn't mean it.

I used to be at a station next door to a halfway house, and every time we put on the siren one of the guys would jump in front of us—like, the voices in his head would tell him to jump in front of the ambulance. And he wasn't trying to die. He was just following his voices, and we'd have to brake really fast as he flung himself into the street and every time I'd have to just yell like "It's just us, Derek! It's just *us* again!" Every day. For years. But I always thought... if you're going to jump, you might as well jump in front of an ambulance. Unless you really really mean it, if you really want to die. Otherwise you might as well jump in front of an ambulance.

Chapter Three

The partner I've done the most shifts with is Amir. Amir is a bit older. He wasn't EMS here when he started. He was a medic for the Armed Forces in Afghanistan, and he is… tough. I asked him about it once—I didn't know if he'd want to talk about it, but we knew each other well—so I asked, after all the bombs and stuff, wasn't it hard? Wasn't it hard… mentally? He actually said it was the rapes that he couldn't deal with, more than the bombs. The bombs are more massive, more overwhelming, but there were a lot of rapes. Amir is my favourite. Amir is totally like… Amir is the *best*. It's a relationship, like it just *IS* one. Amir like… he was my actual partner, like we were a tag-team. We only worked sometimes together, not a regular regular thing, but I guess that's why it turned into a bit of a… it is a romance, like a *non-romance* romance. Some partners are together ten years, fifteen years, and those are work life-partners, those are marriages. They've been through literal fires together. Amir and me weren't really like THAT, I haven't had that. I haven't stuck with anyone. Amir and me were on and off, on and off, six weeks yes, six weeks no. But that made it special when we were on.

Amir… knows he's my favourite. He teases me about it. Says that I like him best. I do. Amir knows how to work, he knows how to be quiet when it's time to be quiet and listen to the patient, he knows how to talk to families, he just *knows* things. He knows how to properly CPR, he knows how to deal with rapes, he knows about burns. He knows. Not all medics know. Sometimes it's like, how did you get here? Don't do that!—*What are you doing*?

Now I'm a Level Three, which is the highest level, so I work swing—wherever I'm needed—and that's really… hit and miss. Sometimes it's with Amir, or another medic like Amir, but sometimes…

Recently I finished two sessions with Harry as my partner. That's six weeks and then another six weeks, and Harry… is like….he's nice. He tries really hard to be nice to me, and maybe if I was a more compassionate person I would find him charming, or like a fun character. But I just can't. He just never… stops. Ever. He never stops talking, he never stops moving, he's always doing something that he doesn't need to be doing. We go to calls and he never ever stops moving, he's like… Tigger all the time, just *bounce bounce bounce*. And it wouldn't bother me that much except it's just… very close quarters. The ambulances are….the space is small, it's *this* much space, and he never stops talking for twelve hours. And… I need to do this really intense thing and make these really clear, important decisions in ten seconds of thinking time, and I have to go over every scenario, and after those moments of doing and thinking, I just want to sit in the ambulance and take those three minutes to be a little bit… quiet. And calm. But he never stops, he never stops at all. He's older than me, so he thinks that he should be in charge. But he's not in charge.

Harry is… dangerous. He has this idea that people can walk things off. Like a football coach. You know, like, "walk it off guys!" A cyclist on Roncesvalles got hit by a car, went through two car windows, and smashed into the road, Harry's reaction was… "well, she's walking, she's OK." WHAT!? No! *She went through two car windows Harry. We need to secure her spine*! He let her sit up, I was so angry. Even though she was OK in the end, except for these five really intense gashes across her face. She was cool about it. She actually DJ'd, so she just started being DJ Scratchface.

On urgent calls I tell Harry to go fast, I talk to him in an urgent tone of voice, so he goes in slow motion. To make a point. That I'm being hysterical. And on calls that are not urgent he goes really fast and shouts so I look apathetic. He scares the shit out of people whose loved one is having, like, a totally standard seizure. I actually think about killing him sometimes, like I have homicidal fantasies.

One time me and Harry were on call to a kindergarten class—little girl is having an asthma attack, hiding under a table across the room—everything's fine, it's very normal. But Harry's RUNNING across the room, for no reason. So another kid gets in the way with a bunch of toys and Harry trips on this toy basket of fruit, face plants right on the tiles, yells "SHIT!" and starts stumbling across the room toward our patient under the table, and now he's fallen he has blood running out of his nose, looks like a monster, and starts yelling at the kids, like "Get Out of the Way! Go go go!" He puts his bleeding face right in front of the little girl having as asthma attack and says "Don't worry, sweetheart—Everything's going to be OK!" I just took over that call, like, come on.

Harry wanted to be a cop, but couldn't make it as a cop, so he's even worse at crime scenes. Always showing off. We had one police shooting up at Finch. And it's a huge deal, obviously, loads of pressure, like I need this call to go *perfectly*. This call needs to be executed one-hundred-percent correctly, 'cause this is one of those calls that you will eventually be describing to a jury.

So I'm in the back, working on keeping this cop from bleeding out, siren's going, it's critical, and I look up and realize that we're going East. We're going to the wrong hospital, we've taken a wrong turn. *HOW?* Tigger has decided to drive us to North York General. But we have a path cleared to Sunnybrook. There are cops all lined up ahead of us blocking intersections. We are supposed to go to the trauma hospital, *Harry*, because it's a trauma.

And I have to scream like "WHAT ARE YOU DOING?! NO! GO SOUTH!" And there's Tigger like "This guy's dead! Go Go Go!"—*BOUNCING!* And the guy's not dead. Calm the fuck down. But Tigger wants to be a hero. But meanwhile we're totally going to somewhere that makes no sense so the news helicopter that is filming us gets the super reassuring sight of an ambulance stopping. And doing a fucking U-turn. With all the sirens still going. Like we, the *ambulance,* got lost going to a *hospital*. Describing that in court made us look super-professional.

We went to a house on the Danforth for an older guy with chest pains. He's like… eighty. Conscious enough to call us, but in bad shape, having a major heart attack. We get there, the guy's in the living room and we come in, door's open, but still we make noise and freak the guy's dog out. It starts barking. I'm trying to put the mask on the old guy to get him some oxygen, and this basset hound is barking really loud, and it's in the way. So yeah, Harry did have to move it. But instead of just being a normal person, and like, picking the whole dog up (it wasn't that big) Harry grabs the dog's collar and drags it across the room. Which isn't safe. That's not a safe way to move a dog, that makes it easy for it to jump up and get your face. Stupid. And it's also shitty for the dog cause Harry's pulling it backwards, God knows why, so the collar is choking it. Not enough to strangle it, probably, but enough to hurt it. And scare it, and provoke it to bite you. Stupid. And this eighty-year-old guy who is having a heart attack sees this and, honest to God, stands up from his chair and starts waving his arms, lunging forward, basically trying to fight Harry. It was a miracle that he could stand but he did it because… he's the dog's person. I get it. He had every symptom of heart failure but still he was ready to fight anyone hurting his dog.

I mean, you can't do your job if the dog's in the way, you do have to do something. But the dog is scared of you. You have to move them sometimes but... Harry is the type of medic who doesn't understand that for some people, protecting their dog is more important than protecting their heart.

Dogs feel things, like loyalty. And fear. The dog thinks you're going to hurt their person. Dogs don't understand what's going on, they don't know why you're there. They're just trying to be protective. The dog is just doing his job and trying to save the person. Just like us.

I also respect cats but cats will eat you. Will eat your body. That happens all the time.

Chapter Four

Once... we got an urgent call, and it was on my street. It's a house right on Pearson, and it's a suicide. This guy cut his wrists, changed his mind, called 911. So then I'm like... *oh no, I am going to know him, it's going to be a neighbour. Shit.* We get there and I do know the house. I know the blue SUV in the driveway, I can picture the guy who lives here. He has a smallish dog that's a mix or something unusual, I'm not sure, and he lives alone and his name is like Jim or... James or... Richard. Maybe. But that's all I knew before but now... if he lives, shit, if he lives he's going to know I know about him killing himself. And whenever I see him around the neighbourhood it's going to be super weird.

We get there and there's all this... shit on the lawn. All this furniture and books and clothes and a treadmill and TVs and a laptop and... there's a twister board and all this tupperware and luggage filled with even more stuff. His house is empty, he's put it all on the lawn and I'm like... yes, this

IS super weird. Even if I didn't know him it would be super weird. We go inside and every room is totally empty, like he's moving or something. And we find the bathroom and yeah, it's my neighbour, it's Jim, or James or whatever... he's in the tub, he's... trying to die, cutting his wrists, and giving up all his possessions. Ridding himself of all the stuff before he leaves the world behind. We take him to the hospital and he's fine. We send him to Psych and he was fine. But then after that, 'cause I'm still living in the same place, he's on his porch a lot drinking coffee when I leave for work. So we do a weird morning nod. Every time I see him I have to nod, like you would nod at somebody you know, at the gym. *"AH yes, hi, good morning, not sure of your name but we met that one time at your suicide!"*

For a moment, ANNA sees something we don't see, and starts to talk to herself, distracted and agitated.

ANNA: Every time I see him I have to nod, to Jim / James... Richard, every time I see him, every time I see him, I know, and he knows, we met that one time at your suicide, every time, we met that one time—

Chapter Five

Suicides are about speed. You have like, thirty seconds sometimes to run in, find the person, what did they do, how did they do it. It's a rush. To get to a call in the ambulance, to arrive at a scene.... Eight Fifty-Nine is the goal, to be kind of simple about it, it's the time that it's supposed to take the ambulance to get somewhere: eight minutes and fifty-nine seconds. And that's why I get angry when the calls come in and we're the closest ones to a scene, and we're fifteen minutes away. It's just like... shit happens, and nothing's perfect, and sometimes the system will mess up but eventually you just think, there are so many people, who might get hurt, who might be critical, there's just so many places and people that might need EMS and there just... it's not that we won't come, we will come, but we might not come in eight minutes and fifty nine seconds. We might not even make eight fifty-nine most of the time. And if you're not fast.... OK, I never felt that the extra time was the deciding factor in what happened to a person, but I have a been a little... close, once and a while. A little too close to call, a little tiny bit unsure, whether it was time that made the person not come back, not make it, that let them bleed out, that let them choke, that let the smoke get in their lungs, or the water, or whatever, or that... sometimes it's the moments you think... like the disappearing man... you think, what happened? What you should have... when I'm *uncertain*. Those are the ones that I think of as bad ones, not actually the ones where the people die, 'cause people will die. Like, EMS is nothing but... at least in school they told us about it like this: EMS is just like a modern funeral director, basically. Funeral directors used to pick people up and bring them to the funeral home. And then they realized that sometimes the people they picked up were still alive! Like, *We weren't supposed to bury that guy! Shit!* So then funeral directors got trained to decide if someone was still alive or not. And then they would drive them to the morgue or the hospital. Left or right. That's still kind of how, I dunno... it's not as simple as that, we don't call it anymore, you need a doctor to call it mostly. But it is still... left or right. Still, that's not the difference between a good call and a bad call. Some people are always going to die. Just not as many if we get there in eight minutes fifty nine. But there are perfect calls, where we do everything, and there are shitty calls when we fuck up.

Chapter Six

The most perfect call I ever did was horrible. A mom forgot her ten-month-old kid in the bath, and he was under water for too long. Classic, typical neglect. Lots of cops. And it was too late. He'd been under too long. It was awful. Parents are both on lots of meth, and they just… can't look after a baby. This is their second kid—the first one got taken away by Children's Aid—and they think they have it together this time, but they fuck up, they get high, they… make a mistake and that's it. It was horrible, it was totally horrible. But it was a perfect call, everyone at the hospital complimented me, said I had done everything, it was a job well done. So there you go. That day was actually… easier. Than working with Harry. Honestly. Because him shouting, bouncing around, I think I might have worked slower. As it was, the ambulance went fast, and the operator asked all the right questions and said all the right things on the phone, and we went to the right place really quickly. Two minutes, eighteen seconds. We went in and I was already thinking in the ambulance, getting all the bits of information I had together so I could get there and assess quickly. And make a decision, and act. And I worked the best I could, the best that a Level 3 works. And I don't worry about that call, it doesn't… resonate.

Chapter Seven

We got a call for asthma and I walk into this house and it was like, a real drug dealer's house. It was a gang-operated crack den, basically. It's immediately just weed, smoke, so much in your face and just…. awful. Scary. Obviously full of illegal shit. This tough gang-member kind of guy is on the floor having a crazy asthma attack, which is… obviously your house is just smoke. Everywhere. The guy's been feeling it all day but he didn't want to go to the hospital because, you know, he's a drug dealer or whatever. He's wheezing on the floor and his brother calls me in. And his brother is holding him in his arms, and I'm like, OK, put him on the floor so I can examine him. And the brother starts flipping out, won't put him down, says the floor is too cold. And I'm like OK, dude, I can help, put him down. But the brother just won't listen, won't be rational, won't do anything and he's swearing at me and he's just calling me every name and I try to tell him I can't do anything like this, put him down. And he's like "save him!" and I'm trying, and he's yelling over and over, and the whole thing is just too much and then right at the moment I'm realizing I forgot my radio in the ambulance and I have no way to get backup and I am alone, he turns to me and says "Bitch, save him. I have a gun." Opens his jacket and he totally does, he does have a gun.

Moment of tension. My cell phone rings. And it's an ambulance sound: my cell phone ring is a siren. So you know: Reeeeooooh.

Guy with the gun looks really freaked out, and then I'm like, oh my God: he thinks it's like a security thing, somehow, he thinks I called the cops without touching my phone. I have to say "No! It's just my phone!" but words didn't... happen. So he puts the brother down, grabs my phone, and I guess he wants to turn it off but he drops it and it opens and I can see it's my mom calling. And now he's actually pointing the gun at me and is like *"Bitch I Am Going To Shoot You."*

Like, Whoah, OK. I can't do anything if you shoot me! Right?!

I am trying to move but I can't and I'm thinking: I'm going to get shot and my mom's going to hear and I probably won't die. He's not aiming at anything much, mostly, like, my shoulder. I guess it's not impossible that he would hit an artery, it's possible, but through the whole time I really assumed I wasn't going to die but I might get a bullet through me and my mom is going to hear and she said being a medic was too dangerous and I don't want her on the phone. She does NOT handle anxiety well. Her stress tolerance is LOW. She will never stop talking about it if she hears me get shot and shit—what if I get shot badly, like what if I get shot in the arm, what if I can't work? They always say not to forget your radio. I'm going to get in so much shit for that— How much will it hurt? I bet it hurts to get shot.

Then the brother just... dies.

It saved me. Asthma death is pretty quick unless you try to reverse it, so the drug dealer guy is way too upset to shoot anyone, and I can get out and call for backup. But now I don't have a cell phone. Fuck cell phones.

Amir was super mad at me about the drug dealer guy. He was like "What the fuck were you doing? It's a crack den. A crack dealer with a gun in a crack den. You shouldn't have gone inside. You're an idiot. You wait outside with your partner. You call for backup. Where was your radio? Why the fuck weren't you carrying your radio? What happened? What's wrong with you?"

When Amir was in Kandahar... he witnessed something. He won't tell me all of it, he can't get through the whole story, but it was something that stood out even in Afghanistan as... especially upsetting. Something about a mother and her kid, but I don't know what happened to them exactly, he won't tell me.

When he's under high high pressure, on a really bad call—his eyes will glaze over and he'll lose himself, lose his focus, get over-stimulated, his hands will shake. Just on a really bad call, not a lot. I try not to mind because otherwise, Amir is the best. And then while he's calming down, when the call's over, I can hear him talking to himself a bit, and I know he's back in Afghanistan, with the mother and her kid. And then he'll turn to me and suddenly say right to my face "*nobody helped her, nobody did anything. Everyone saw and nobody helped her—*"

He said he felt like the only one who couldn't cope. He felt like a loser for having nightmares and asking to be sent home. But he had to because after what he saw, he was bad at his job. Sometimes things happen and then suddenly: you can't work, you can't focus, you can't make safe decisions, you go places without taking precautions. You lose yourself in the middle of an important decision. You become reckless, because... you're being haunted.

Chapter Eight

It was called in as an unknown, an unconscious woman, found by her neighbour, breathing. But we did figure sexual assault. And that's always kind of... unhappy for me, for most of us, it's a certain kind of... reaction. But ultimately not totally... uncommon. So I get there and see that it's a female, maybe forty or a little younger maybe, she's lying on her back, she's unconscious, she's naked—though actually a lot of people are naked when we get there. Accidents happen a lot in showers, or people get really freaked out like they're choking or panicking so they just take all their clothes off. So this is not an immediate alarm bell for me, so far. Except that you can tell... she looks bad, like, drugs probably. But she's OK, I think, at first glance, except that she's... poor. Bad teeth and just... nobody with money ever looks like this. But actually then...

um, this was a little hard to... I felt like there was something wrong. I knew something was wrong so I'm thinking, rape victim, maybe, like I just know there's something off. Suddenly I see all the blood all through the mattress, I can't tell where it's from... but I look at her closer and then I realize what it is. I don't know how I didn't see it right away but my brain didn't... process that her arm, right in the middle of the top part, is actually lying next to her about half an inch away from her shoulder. Like, physically separated, from her. And so then I notice it's the same deal with her other arm, she has been cut away. At the arms, on both sides. And that was actually quite... I'm usually pretty good but that was quite... because she's been drugged, I'm pretty sure, so she can't move, and I think that was... I think about that one sometimes. Just because, the person had cut them away from her, and then put them back so they looked attached, but they weren't. And I think about that because... she lived so... I think about that one, I had a really bad, like... that's the only time I lost myself, like, physically, at a scene. I just looked at her arms and realized and then I threw up, like, I projectile vomited in this woman's bathroom. And that is not normal. I do not get freaked out by things. That never happens.

And somehow it all started to be different, like, physically I couldn't take it, I started really hating it, the whole deal, just 'cause I just hated the shit. The physical shit and the vomit and the blood. For a while I was doing calls, acting totally cool, obviously I have to be totally okay. And then after I would think about the call, and the woman who had her arms cut off, and I would start to feel these tremors, this shaking feeling through my fingers and hands until I couldn't use them and nothing would change it. I even went to Psych and he says, "Do you feel traumatized?" He really isn't very good. And I was like, OK, let's do this: yes I feel traumatized.

That was bad, that was really bad.

Me and Amir were six weeks on when that happened. We'd been working pretty hard for a while and I was feeling like, less, sort of… I wasn't crying I was… not feeling anything. I started getting this thing where I couldn't ever just be still. I didn't want my thoughts in the ambulance. I didn't want quiet anymore. I couldn't stand the breaks anymore. In the moments between calls or whatever I couldn't stop moving. I was kind of bouncy and I kept sort of making stupid mistakes and I just wanted to tire myself out but I never could. I never felt like I could slow down or rest or sleep. I just kept thinking and moving and bouncing and doing things, just bounce bounce bounce out of control—

Chapter Nine

It's four in the morning. Me and Amir are just leaving the Emerg and I'm waiting while Amir gets a coffee from the machine, and this man and woman run inside the hospital and they have a child with them and they yell at me… DO SOMETHING. Their kid isn't breathing. They're all… surprised that their baby isn't breathing… they look surprised…. but it's obvious they'd just… they didn't feed the baby, and now the baby is dying. I'm working and working doing so much CPR and then the doctors come and take it and… I didn't ask anyone if the baby died but that was… obvious. I don't want to look right at the parents but I do and the woman has these glazed-over eyes and I think sort of vaguely that she's probably on meth. And then…

I look through the Emerg doors at the parents and just as they're closing…

...I recognize them. This is the woman who forgot her ten-month-old in the bathtub. How are you surprised? How is it you're surprised every time?

I hear him say to her and I hear him say to her... don't worry, don't worry, we'll have another one.

So suddenly I'm through the doors and I am shaking this woman and yelling and I'm making her neck go pretty far front to back and I'm yelling STOP IT DON'T DO THIS AGAIN DON'T HAVE ANOTHER ONE DON'T DO THIS AGAIN YOU HAVE TO STOP—

I felt Amir spill his coffee on me and he was yelling "GO HOME. What are you doing?" He grabbed my arm and yelled at me, "Anna what are you doing? This isn't your job. STOP. You have to STOP. You're bad at your job now, Anna. You're bad at your job"—

They said I assaulted this woman and... I know I shook her and scared her. I didn't do any harm, any real damage. She's fine. But yes, they called the cops in. And that's what they call... that is assault.

I got fired.

Chapter Ten

In the last few weeks, I've gone to lots of places. Not to see the woman with no arms. But I went to Castle Frank to listen to the Ballad of the Missing Man. Then I went to the hardware store on Kingston where we saved the guy who was ODing on coke at eight in the morning. And to the 401 exit where I delivered that baby, and the swimming pool where the lifeguard wanted to kill himself but then he was happy we showed up. I went to the elementary school that called us where I restarted this kid's heart who choked on a candy on Halloween. He was dressed up as Snoopy and his mom ran up to me afterwards and tried to give me fifty dollars as a thank you. Later she sent me an invitation to go to his bar mitzvah. A part of me wishes I'd gone to that, actually.

I went to High Park and figured out how the guy climbed the tallest tree to hang himself at the top; there are these grooves in the side you can get up if you really want to, and there's a great view over the water. The trick is, you can't think about how you're going to get back down. I went to the Scotia building, I went to a couple of swimming pools, I went to the old age homes, I went to the park with my first rape case—they've put in lights now—and I went to the old station. Then to the building with my first hanging, my first fire, I couldn't remember most of the houses but I did go to the yoga studio and the first really sad miscarriage which was at the Eaton Centre in the maternity section of the Gap. And then I went down to the Beaches, which is where we got called for that guy who said he had a bomb a couple of years ago. He didn't really have a bomb. People are liars. I went to the YMCA on Gerrard where we found the Wolf Guy with the broken arm—the same guy who flagged us down that one time. We didn't realize it was him at first. The YMCA just called us in for a guy with a broken arm and it had been broken for a while so we were like, fine, OK, we just need to take this guy to the hospital. Amir got him in the ambulance and asked how it happened, how'd he break it, and he's like "There's an infestation of wolves in my room, Toronto has a huge wolf problem that nobody in the government gives a shit about," something, something… and I was like… Oh my God. Wolves. I recognized his red baseball cap… he's the guy who flagged us down. On the way to Castle Frank the day our jumper disappeared! He had a broken arm, it's the same guy. The guy we told, like, man, go to the hospital. *You still haven't gone?!* He made us lose our jumper and he hadn't even gone to the hospital.

I went to the restaurant where I had my first pretend heart attack. It's a thing, you know, people don't want to pay their bills at restaurants so they fake a heart attack. I remember the first time it happened I was so confused and Amir was like… "See?… People are terrible. There's always a chance they're faking it." Amir always says that about every weird call: "See, people are terrible. People are terrible. They just want to be rescued."

Chapter Eleven

These last few weeks were about planning for me, and I've been happier because I knew that I was making a plan and setting things in motion like finding someone to take care of my mom, and writing a letter to Amir to say I was sorry. I used to have more people that I would need to write letters to, but now… it sneaks up on you but I've just been working and I don't see anyone and then… you realize you don't have any people anymore—

If you don't really want to die, if you want to be rescued, you might as well jump in front of an ambulance. I thought about jumping in front of a subway. That's very certain, very effective. So long as you go to the left side, the side the train enters on, so the train hits right away, full speed, and keeps going fully over your body. Not at the far end, where the train is slowed down so the impact might not suck you underneath, might just hit you and hurt a lot. The right way to do it is at the end the train enters from, so the train goes fully over you, and that would have been my first choice, I think.

But I didn't want to leave behind a mess for medics to clean up. They would probably know me. And even worse… I just felt like it would be Harry on the call. I don't know why, but I just had a feeling it would be Harry on the call. And I hate him. And he would be gathering bits of me, finding my leg or my arm and waving them in the air, showing off that he found a body part, and I didn't want that. It would have been my first choice to jump though. There'd be a moment in the air—

Chapter Twelve

I decided to use pills. That's quiet, and pretty clean. I've had a prescription for Valium for ages and mixing Tylenol and Valium with alcohol is a very sure thing, if you live alone and there's no chance anyone's going to find you, and if you calculate the dose right. Then it will work for sure. You have to plan if you really don't want anyone to save you.

Today coming home from the pharmacy on Roncey I walked by my neighbour's house (The Jim/James… Richard… guy who tried to kill himself). I walk by the house a lot. It's near me. I see it all the time, but today for a moment I think: I'm hallucinating. I've been thinking about the bottle of Valium I just got and I think—*you're hallucinating, Anna, you have suicide on the brain, you've gotta be hallucinating*—but I'm not, it's real: Jim/James/Richard has put all his shit on the lawn again. TV, laptops, treadmill AND StairMaster… bed, table, a bookshelf with books in it, lamps, board games… all over the lawn, just like last time. His weird garage-sale funeral with all the shit on the lawn is happening again. Fuck. Again! Now… I have to see if he's killing himself again. I don't want to go inside but… It's like he's waving a flag. A weird *"I'm killing myself!"* flag.

I should have been a veterinarian. People are just… terrible. We all just want to die, it's a huge problem.

People everywhere are trying to die or practically trying to kill themselves and being totally reckless and ruining everything and there's only so much I can personally do about that, right? At a certain point is this really my job? I guess it's not my job anymore—

I did go in and… It was a suicide, he bled everywhere. He's in the bathtub. Whatever. And I was about to… do my thing, you know. Save him, or whatever, I don't know. I mean, it's so clear he doesn't actually want to die. But it's not like I can start punishing him for crying wolf right? That's not my place, no matter how many times he does it. I'm not God, I'm just a medic. I mean, I'm not a medic. I'm not a medic, I'm just a person. But I'm about to stop the bleeding and drain the water from the tub, I see him still conscious, looking right at me, just like he does when I see him in the mornings on his porch, and I nod at him again like: *"Oh yes, you, we met that one time at your suicide."* And I am draining the tub so he doesn't drown and he starts to lose consciousness. Like now he can relax because I'm here. And I am about to work on his vitals but then…

I saw the dog. In the hallway. Kind of an unusual dog, I'd seen him walking it before. A mix or something. A pet dog. But this guy in the bath… He's obviously like, purposely, over a long time just kicked and beat and starved his dog. It's covered in its own fluids and totally starved thin, just ribs sticking out and the dog definitely has a really bad, really painful eye infection. He's just got pus coming out of his eye and can't even see anymore, he's just a lump of jagged bones, he's barely even… aware. This guy has let this dog live in its own shit, it's covered in its own fluids. And then I saw that really the worst part I didn't notice at first, he'd… this guy had like, this guy has taken a pair of scissors and cut the dog's tongue down the middle. It's a clean cut but I couldn't take that I could not stomach that. And then I look at this little, awful loser of a man. Like, who gives a shit about his problems? I don't. I don't give a shit about his problems, his issues or his depression, why he wants to die, like, I just… Fuck him. I don't care about you, you can.… I looked at the situation and I saw that the dog was bleeding from this deep gash in his mouth, that his person, this so-called person had actually clipped the dog's tongue before he tried to kill himself. And it's not very likely to work, when you cut your own wrists, it's not very effective, a lot of people do it and they don't mean it and it doesn't work, because we stop it from working.

The guy's still conscious… and he's lying all… posed… wrists out… Waiting for me to come in and change what's supposed to happen to him and giving me this look, this expectant look and lifting his wrist up towards me, palm out, like a request.

…I took stock of the situation and picked. The most vital thing to address.

The dog was going to bleed out so I used a towel, cut and tie, it's hard with a dog usually because they move but this one is still, putting its head to the side to let the blood drain out, stopping itself from choking, just very quietly trying to save itself and—I hold the dog and clean its eye and—I chose the dog. Because that's not murder. That's suicide. He did it to himself. He killed himself. I did the best work I've ever done on that dog's vitals and… the dog's not going to tell anyone. Even if the dog could talk, his tongue was split open. So. I didn't kill him. I just… didn't save him and that's fine, you know, that's—

SHIT. What am I supposed to do now?

Chapter Thirteen

ANNA holds up the landline she has found in the house.

She dials three distinct numbers.

DISPATCHER: 911. What's your emergency?... Do you require fire? Police? Ambulance?

ANNA: Ambulance.

DISPATCHER: What is your emergency?...

ANNA: There's a guy and I think he's dead. I let the water out but I should have stopped the bleeding—

DISPATCHER: OK, what's the address?

ANNA: 151 Pearson Street. I need an ambulance.

DISPATCHER: 151 Pearson. Help is on its way. They'll be there in a moment—

ANNA: It's a severe hemorrhage. Man, 50-60 years of age, slashed his wrists in the tub... unconscious, he's in the basement. 151 Pearson Street, Roncesvalles and Dundas, one-way going east, It's a Delta call... are you coming?

DISPATCHER: Don't worry the ambulance is on its way—151 Pearson, that's a house right?

ANNA: Yeah, it's a house. Use the back door. The front door is blocked off, the back door is open. The man is in the bathroom in the basement, medications by the sink, he has a history of suicides. The door is unlocked.

DISPATCHER: OK... is there anyone else in the house?

ANNA: I'm by myself.

DISPATCHER: And do you have any pets?

ANNA: I have a dog.

Chapter Fourteen

ANNA addresses us again.

ANNA: I went to Psych after the woman with no arms and Dr. Wincheski was eating this stupid cupcake and he just said… *have you ever considered getting a dog?* At the time I was like… you're stupid. Were you even listening? But this dog is different. It's all fucked up. Who would want it? But I do. I like wolves, I mean—I like dogs.

That guy we picked up from the YMCA with the broken arm kept talking like "The wolves were howling at me! Toronto has a huge wolf problem and nobody in the government gives a shit about it—" and we kept saying "No wolves, there are no wolves—how did you break your arm?" We kept asking him why he didn't just go to the hospital, but he's just on and on "the municipal system is not effectively wolf-barricaded, not the bridges, not even the subways." So we're taking him to the hospital, he's still just chatting away to himself like "wolves everywhere, wolves in the station, what was I supposed to do? I called 911 but the howling was too loud and I couldn't take it anymore, you took so damn long I jumped in front of the train!"

….You took so damn long, I jumped in front of the train.

Oh my God. He told us, he told us—

"I called 911 but the wolves were howling too loudly and I couldn't stand it any more… I couldn't fucking take it anymore so I jumped in front of the train."

He was the jumper. That guy was the Castle Frank Jumper. The disappearing man! Oh my God, how did we not know he was the jumper!?!

He must have jumped at the far end, at the wrong end—

He must have hit the front of the train, but it's not too bad because the train's already slowed a lot 'cause it's mostly in the station, so he just breaks his arm. And there's an announcement to evacuate the station… so he does just… evacuate his own suicide. Then he walks along Bloor, sees us driving by, siren on. He flags us down, says: "I have a broken arm!"And we stop and because of that then we think we missed our jumper but—

Oh my God, I found the jumper. Oh my God, I have to tell Amir I found the jumper.

I have to tell Amir I got a dog.

Sirens. Ambulance arrives. ANNA talks to her dog:

ANNA: Come on! Come here, dog! Let's go! Don't be scared, it's just a siren, don't worry. Don't be scared. It's just some people, don't be scared. Come on. I know, I know, but that's OK, I know, people are scary. People are terrifying, they're just terrifying but don't be scared.

ANNA exits with her dog.

The End.